MENOTTI

RICERCARE AND TOCCATA   FOR THE PIANO

On a Theme from The Old Maid and the Thief

EDITED BY ALBERT MENDOZA

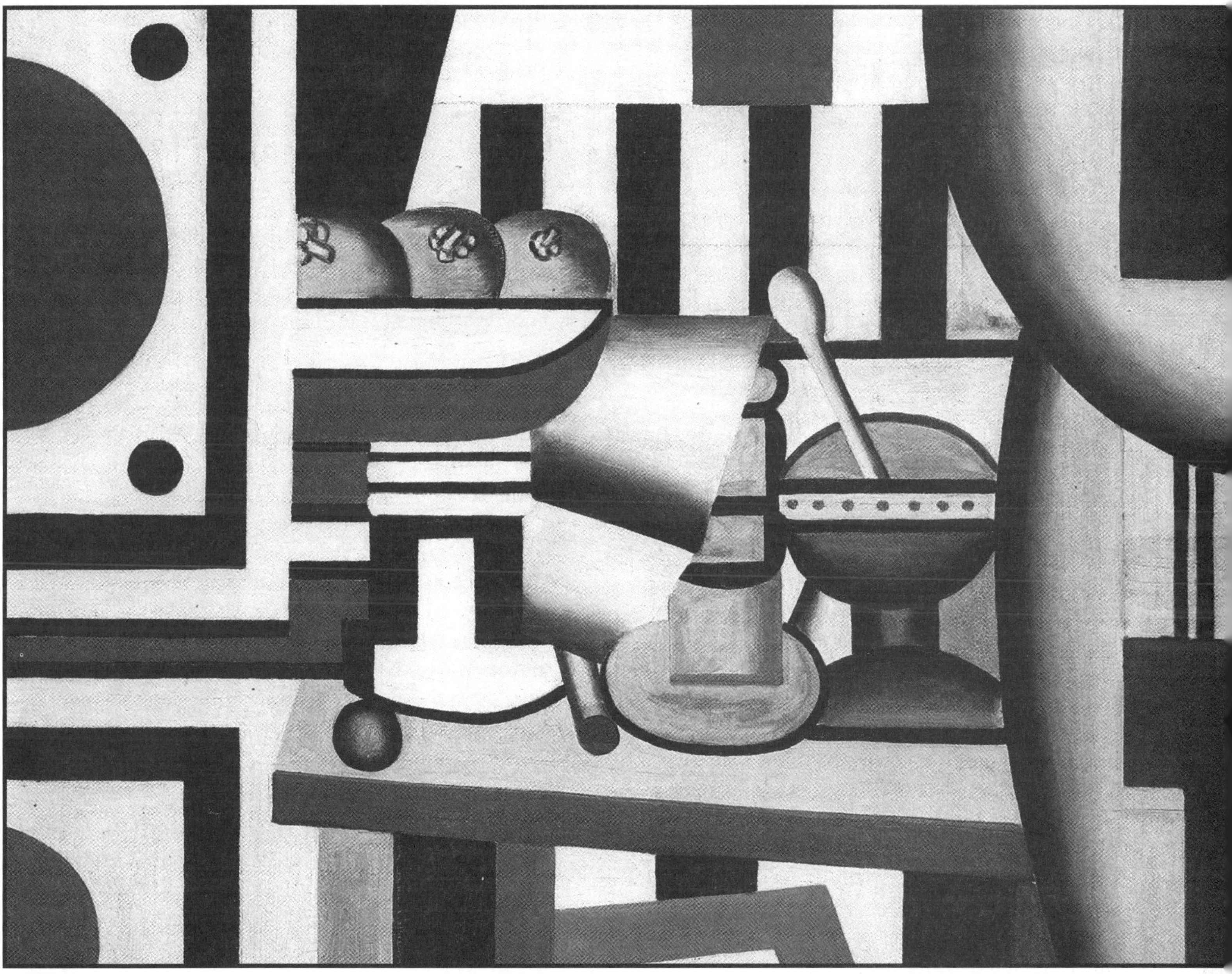

AN ALFRED MASTERWORK EDITION

Alfred Music
P.O. Box 10003
Van Nuys, CA 91410-0003
alfred.com

Cover art: Composition de poires (Composition of pears) *(1923)*
by Fernand Léger (French, 1881–1955)

GIAN CARLO MENOTTI

CONTENTS

Foreword

ABOUT THE COMPOSER

Gian Carlo Menotti, Italian-American composer and librettist, was born in Cadegliano-Viconago, Italy, on July 7, 1911, and died in Monte Carlo, Monaco, on February 1, 2007. He studied at the Milan Conservatory and the Curtis Institute of Music, where he subsequently taught. At Curtis, Menotti studied composition with Rosario Scalero and began a long career of writing operas, first in Italian and later in English. He also wrote his own libretti, two for American composer Samuel Barber (1910–1981), his lifelong companion. Several of Menotti's operas were written for radio or for television. In addition, Menotti wrote ballets, choral works, cantatas, a Mass, a violin concerto, a piano concerto, a triple concerto, a song cycle, a suite for two cellos, three solo piano works, and several other unpublished works.

ABOUT THE MUSIC

Menotti published three works for solo piano: *Poemetti per Maria Rosa: 12 Pieces for Children* (1937), piano selections based on the popular television opera *Amahl and the Night Visitors* (1951), and *Ricercare and Toccata on a Theme from "The Old Maid and the Thief"* (1953).

Menotti's *The Old Maid and the Thief*

Following the success of Menotti's opera *Amelia al ballo (Amelia Goes to the Ball)*, NBC commissioned Menotti for a radio opera. The result was Menotti's first opera in English, *The Old Maid and the Thief*. The successful one-act opera premiered on April 22, 1939, with Alberto Erede conducting the NBC Symphony Orchestra, and was later adapted for the stage.

The opera is composed in *opera buffa* (comic opera) style with 14 discrete scenes rather than a through-composed form, a format well-suited for radio. The plot concerns Bob, a handsome beggar, who wanders one day to the doorstep of town spinster Miss Todd. Laetitia, the young maid of the house, convinces Miss Todd to talk to him. Taken by his good looks, they convince him to stay the night for rest and a meal. He captivates them with his wit and storytelling, leading them the next morning to persuade him to stay for another week. Confusion later ensues when Bob is mistaken for an escaped thief and suspicions are raised in the town. Frightened by the news but helpless to Bob's charm and desperate to win his affections, Miss Todd steals money from her neighbors and alcohol from a local liquor store to give to Bob. After a confrontation with him, Bob reveals that he is not the thief everyone suspects him to be. As an argument unfolds between them, Miss Todd threatens to turn him over to the authorities even though he has done nothing wrong. When she goes to get the police, Laetitia convinces Bob to run away with her. They flee, but only after snatching up Miss Todd's valuables—including her car—leaving her with nothing.

In a 1993 dissertation, Sylvia Watkins Ryan explains how Menotti derived a solo piano piece from this opera:

> Twelve years after the successful radio premiere in 1939 of *The Old Maid and the Thief*, Menotti selected a bold three-measure motto theme from the opera's third scene as the germ for his most advanced piano composition. *Ricercare and Toccata on a Theme from "The Old Maid and the Thief"* was composed in 1951 and premiered on November 1 of that same year in Town Hall by Ania Dorfmann, to whom it was dedicated.[1]

---

[1] Sylvia Watkins Ryan, "The Solo Piano Music of Gian-Carlo Menotti: A Pedagogical and Performance Analysis" (DMA diss., University of Oklahoma, 1993), 103–104.

RICERCARE AND TOCCATA
On a Theme from *The Old Maid and the Thief*

Edited by Albert Mendoza

In the 16th century, *ricercare* were popular keyboard pieces that were free in form and displayed the improvisatory talents of the performers. These pieces had the same function as preludes as they often preceded another accompanying work. In this spirit, Menotti incorporates common elements of early ricercares into his *Ricercare:* an exploration of a theme or subject through fugue-like writing, elaborate coloratura-like flourishes, distinct sections with contrasting textures and pauses at the end of each section, and flamboyant display of technique. In contrast to the sectional nature of the *Ricercare*, the *Toccata* progresses in perpetual motion in a steady 16th-note rhythm pitted against mostly quarter notes and eighth notes. Within these rhythms, Menotti creates moods from humorous to lyrical. Contrasts are achieved through dramatic dynamic changes, varied articulation, and capricious movement across the different registers of the keyboard. The *Ricercare* and the *Toccata* are based on the following expanding-interval theme:

Opera score, scene III ("Bob's Bedroom"), mm. 1–3

In the *Toccata* the theme is quoted directly, while in the *Ricercare* the theme occurs lyrically in C minor. Different treatments of this one theme produce two strikingly dissimilar, yet related, movements. Many measures from the original opera reduction are incorporated verbatim into the *Toccata*.

FORM

The *Ricercare* and *Toccata* can be divided into the following sections for the purpose of analysis or rehearsal. Other sectional divisions are possible.

Ricercare: section I (C minor) = mm. 1–10; II (C minor) = 11–25; III (B minor) = 26; IV (F-sharp minor, B minor) = 27–34; V (B minor) = 35–43; VI (D pedal, D Major) = 44–46.

Toccata: Introduction = 1–3; section I = 4–16; II = 17–35; III = 36–57; IV = 58–73; V = 74–86; VI = 87–102; VII = 103–119.

EDITORIAL CONSIDERATIONS

Metronome marks: Suggested metronome marks are given in parentheses. Maintaining a consistent tempo appropriate for all sections within the *Ricercare* is important. For the *Toccata*, notice the original tempo is *Allegretto mosso*—with motion, but not too fast.

Fingering: All fingering in this edition is editorial and can be adapted to the needs of the performers. Occasionally, alternative fingerings are given in parentheses.

Pedaling: Pedaling is editorial unless otherwise noted. Performers can use pedal in the *Ricercare* to help create the *sempre legato* sound indicated in measure 1; however, care should be taken to avoid blurring the distinct voices. To this end, half pedaling is often the most effective pedaling technique. In the *Toccata*, at measure 17 and similar measures, the *sonoro* (sonorous) sound can be projected and the difficulty of the overlapping voices can be avoided in the following manner:

Articulations and dynamics: Articulations and dynamics match the first edition. A few editorial suggestions are given in parentheses.

SOURCES CONSULTED

Menotti, Gian Carlo. *The Old Maid and the Thief: A Grotesque Opera in 14 Scenes* (vocal score). New York: Franco Colombo, Inc., 1943.

Menotti, Gian Carlo. *Ricercare and Toccata on a Theme from "The Old Maid and the Thief"* (first edition). New York: G. Ricordi & Co., 1953.

This edition is dedicated to Kevin Fitz-Gerald,
for years of musical and pianistic inspiration.

For Ania Dorfmann

Ricercare and Toccata

On a Theme from *The Old Maid and the Thief*

Ricercare

Gian Carlo Menotti
(1911–2007)

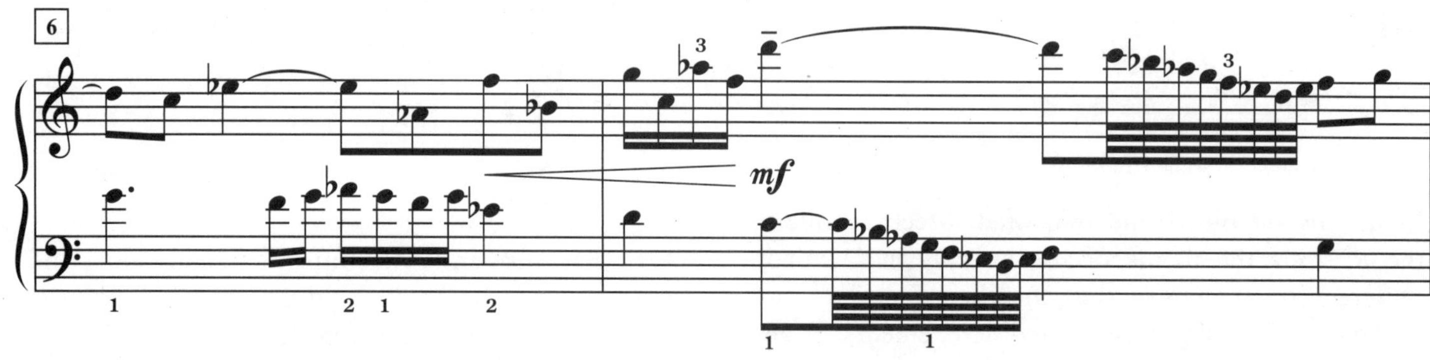

26
liberamente
pedal ad lib.
(leggiero)
tr
(< >)
5-3
(cresc.)
(f
< >
< > < >
27
a tempo
rit.
mf
30
32
f

ⓐ Play the rolls gently and *on the beat:*

ⓑ Change the pedal almost imperceptibly and listen carefully to sustain only the appropriate voices.

Toccata

ff sonoro
espress. e legato
pp
mf
f sonoro
p
f
8va

36
ff
sonoro
il basso molto marcato
39
mf
mf
42
f
ff
45
sempre sonoro
48
51

53
55
(3)
58
mf secco e con umorismo
61
ff
64
mp
67
LH over

p
mf
cantando
1/2

83
85
dim.
87
p
cresc. poco a poco
89
91
f
f secco
93
sonoro

(a) This note is a G in the first edition; however, see measure 33.

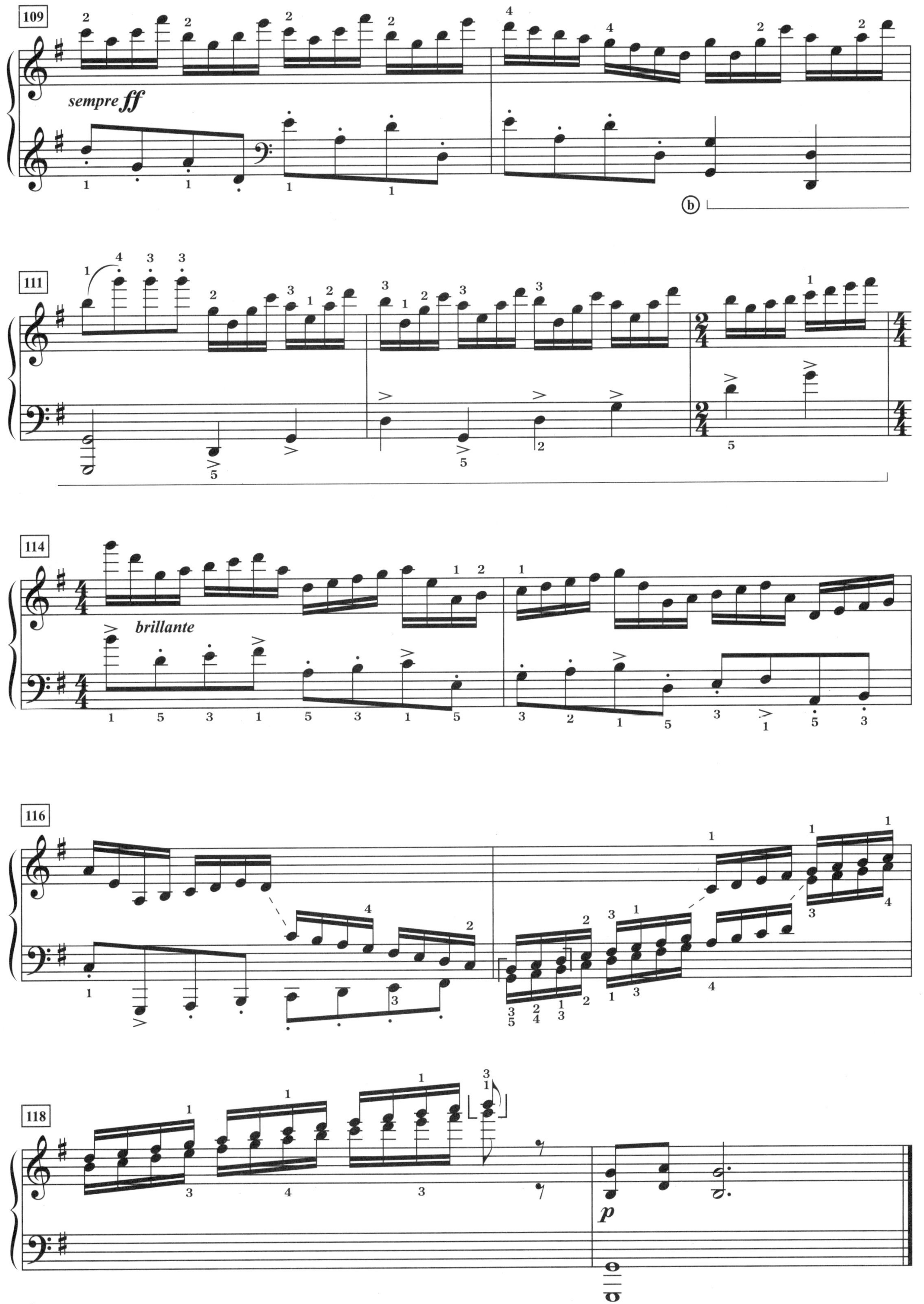

(b) The pedaling in measures 110–113 is Menotti's.